Artists in Their Time

Vincent van Gogh

Jen Green

Franklin Watts
A Division of Scholastic Inc.
New York Toronto London Auckland Sydney
Mexico City New Delhi Hong Kong
Danbury, Connecticut

First published in 2002 by
Franklin Watts
96 Leonard Street
London EC2A 4XD

First American edition published
in 2002 by Franklin Watts
A Division of Scholastic Inc.
90 Sherman Turnpike
Danbury, CT 06816

Series Editor: Adrian Cole
Editor: Jill A. Laidlaw
Series Designer: Mo Choy
Art Director: Jonathan Hair
Picture Researcher: Kathy Lockley

A CIP catalog record for this title
is available from the Library of Congress.

ISBN 0-531-12238-7 (Lib. Bdg.)
ISBN 0-531-16648-1 (Pbk.)

Printed in Hong Kong, China

Acknowledgements

AKG London: 6B, 9B. Tom Ang: Robert Harding Picture Library: 39B. British Library, London:
Bridgeman Art Library: 16T. Pearl Bucknall: Robert Harding Picture Library: 34T. © CAP-Viollet:
28T. Christie's Images, London: Bridgeman Art Library: 11B. Courtauld Institute Gallery, Somerset
House, London: Bridgeman Art Library: 27. Fogg Art Museum, Harvard University Art Museums,
USA. Bequest from the Collection of Maurice Wertheim, Class 1906: Bridgeman Art Library: 26B.
Glasgow Art Gallery & Museum, Scotland: Bridgeman Art Library: 15. Glasgow Museums: Art
Gallery & Museum, Kelvingrove: 12B. Haags Gemeentemuseum, Netherlands: Bridgeman Art Library:
10. Hulton Archive: 8. Simon Harris: Robert Harding Picture Library: 36B. Erich Lessing/AKG
London: 18B. ©. LL-Viollet: 11T. Musee du Louvre, Paris: Bridgeman Giraudon: 39T. Musee
Marmotton, Paris: Bridgeman Giraudon: 14B. Museum of Modern Art, New York: Artothek: 31.
Nasjonalgalleriet, Oslo: Erich Lessing/AKG London: 40. National Gallery, London: Erich
Lessing/AKG London: 14T; Bridgeman Art Library: 21. National Museum & Gallery of Wales, Cardiff:
Bridgeman Art Library: 36, 37 © ND-Viollet: 16B. Oeffentliche Kunstsammlung, Basel: Bridgeman
Art Library: 40. Musee d'Orsay, Paris: Bridgeman: 22R, 26T, 33. Philadelphia Museum of Art: Bequest
of Lisa Norris Elkins/Photo by: Joe Mikuliak, 1994: 28B. Phillips Collection, Washington DC:
Bridgeman Giraudon/Lauros: 18T. Private Collection: Bridgeman Art Library: 17, 35. Pushkin
Museum, Moscow: Artothek: 25T; Bridgeman Art Library: 32R. Walter Rawlings: Robert Harding
Picture Library: 41B: Rijksmuseum, Amsterdam: AKG London: 7. Rijksmuseum Kroeller-Mueller,
Otterlo; Erich Lessing/AKG London: 29, 30B. Bridgeman Art Library: 9T. Stedelijk Museum,
Amsterdam: AKG London: 20T. Van Gogh Museum, Amsterdam: 42. Van Gogh Museum,
Amsterdam: AKG London: 6T, 13, 24, 38 Artothek: 23. Bridgeman Art Library: 19, 20B. ©
Collection Viollet: 12T, 22L, 25B, 30T, 32L.

Whilst every attempt has been made to clear copyright
should there be any inadvertent omission please apply
in the first instance to the publisher regarding rectification.

Contents

Who Was Vincent van Gogh?

The Dutch painter Vincent van Gogh (1853-90) is one of the world's most famous artists. During his career, however, very few people knew his work, and he only ever sold one painting. He was often alone and frequently had fits of illness and depression – yet he is now one of the world's best-loved artists, and his pictures are recognized as masterpieces.

BEGINNINGS

Vincent van Gogh was born on March 30, 1853, in Groot-Zundert in the southern Netherlands. His father, Theodorus van Gogh (1822-85), was the local clergyman and his mother Anna (1819-1907) was a strong and energetic pastor's wife. After Vincent, Theodorus and Anna had five other children: Anna, Theodorus (Theo), Elisabetha, Willemina, and Cornelis. Van Gogh's younger brother Theo would be a close friend for life.

▲ Van Gogh in 1866, at the age of 13, while at boarding school.

◀ The building in the center of this photograph is the presbytery, the house that the van Gogh family lived in. Both Vincent and Theo were born here, Vincent in the room on the first floor with the flag sticking out of the window.

TIMELINE ▶

March 30, 1853	May 1, 1857	1861-64	1864-68	July 30, 1869	May 1873
Vincent van Gogh born in the village of Groot-Zundert in the southern Netherlands.	Theodorus (Theo) van Gogh born.	Van Gogh attends the local school.	Van Gogh attends boarding school.	Van Gogh starts work at the Hague branch of art dealers Goupil & Co.	Van Gogh is transferred to the Goupil & Co. London office.

Vincent van Gogh grew up in the small community of Groot-Zundert. He loved to roam the misty, flat countryside around the village, and often sketched local scenes. He went to the village school until the age of 11, when he was sent to boarding school. He missed his family and familiar surroundings and did not do well during his time studying away from home. During the school holidays, van Gogh continued to make sketches. His drawings showed talent, but his parents did not encourage him to become an artist. Instead, it was decided that he should become an art dealer, like his Uncle Vincent, known in the family as Uncle Cent.

MOVING TO LONDON

Van Gogh became quite successful at Uncle Cent's company, Goupil & Co. In 1873, after four years, the firm transferred him to their branch in London. Van Gogh was enthusiastic about life in London, with its many galleries, parks, and museums, and he particularly liked the National Gallery. However, the extreme poverty he saw in the great city began to upset him.

He fell in love with a young woman named Eugenie Loyer, whose mother owned the lodgings where he was staying. Unfortunately Eugenie did not feel the same way about van Gogh. So, feeling rejected and lonely, surrounded by poverty in a foreign city, van Gogh turned to religion.

DEALING IN ART

In 1869, when van Gogh was 16, Uncle Cent got him a job at the art dealers where he worked. The company, called Goupil & Co., had an office in The Hague, the capital of the Netherlands. In the city, van Gogh could visit impressive museums and galleries including the Royal Picture Gallery. There he could see the work of great Dutch artists such as Rembrandt (1606-69) and Jan Vermeer (1632-75). Van Gogh was excited by his new job and the bustle of buying and selling works of art. In 1872 he began to exchange letters with his brother Theo. Theo was four years younger than van Gogh and still at school, but later he also joined Goupil & Co. The brothers' correspondence, which was to continue throughout van Gogh's life, is a rich source of information about the artist's life, work, and feelings.

▲ *The Militia Company of Captain Frans Banning Cocq,* 1642, **Rembrandt.** This dramatic picture is also known as The Night Watch. Van Gogh would have seen it when visiting the Trippenhuis (now called the Rijksmuseum) in Amsterdam. We know from van Gogh's letters to Theo that he thought Rembrandt was a great artist. In a letter he told his brother that he could sit in front of one of Rembrandt's paintings for ten years with only a crust of bread to eat and be perfectly happy.

Helping the Poor

In London, van Gogh gradually became disillusioned with the world of art dealing. As his early enthusiasm wore off, he confessed to Theo that he had begun to see art dealing as "a form of organized fraud." In 1875, he was transferred to the Goupil & Co. office in Paris, but his employers found working with him very difficult. The following year van Gogh, now 23, was dismissed. He had left work at Christmas, the busiest time of year, without asking permission.

▲ The National Gallery in London, around 1870. Van Gogh loved the National Gallery's fine collection of paintings but was shocked at the contrasts between rich and poor people in the city (see below).

The young man returned to England, where he began working as an assistant teacher of French, German, and arithmetic, at a school in Kent. After a few months, he tried his hand as a social worker and then as a part-time preacher in West London.

STUDYING FOR THE CHURCH

In 1877 van Gogh returned to the Netherlands to work as a clerk in a bookshop. He felt that his Christian faith was getting stronger and he began to form a plan. He wrote to Theo, "there are no professions in the world other than those of schoolmaster and clergyman." He decided he had a calling to be a priest and began to study for the church. He tried twice – in Amsterdam and Brussels – to enter a university to study theology, but was rejected each time.

▲ A poor woman in London, 1870s.

TIMELINE ▶

May 1875	January 1876	Summer 1876	Jan-Apr 1877	May 1877	1878	Dec 1878-Aug 1879
Van Gogh is transferred to the Goupil & Co. Paris office.	Van Gogh is dismissed from Goupil & Co.	Van Gogh works as an assistant teacher, a social worker, and a preacher.	Van Gogh works as a bookshop clerk in Dordecht, the Netherlands.	Van Gogh studies to read theology at the University of Amsterdam but fails the entrance exam.	Van Gogh studies to enter religious college in Brussels but fails the exam.	Van Gogh works as a lay preacher in the Borinage, a mining community.

◀ *Miners' Wives*, 1881. Van Gogh's picture of miners' wives struggling to carry sacks of coal home is very atmospheric – you can almost feel the weight of the coal on the women's backs.

PREACHING TO THE MINERS

Thwarted in his efforts to study for the priesthood, van Gogh now decided to go and help poor people directly. He took a job as a lay, or unqualified, preacher in the Borinage, a poor coal-mining region on the border between France and Belgium. Working conditions in the mines were dangerous, and the miners' families had barely enough money for food and clothes. Van Gogh's heart went out to these people. He was determined to help them in any way he could. He shared the miners' lives and joined them when they went on strike. He gave away most of his clothes and even the money that Theo, still at Goupil's, had begun to send him. But van Gogh was so eager that his employers became worried. In 1879 he was dismissed again.

A TURNING POINT

Having tried his hand as an art dealer, teacher, social worker, preacher, and clerk, van Gogh was out of work again. For the next year, he lived as a wandering preacher, walking the roads in all types of weather and sleeping in barns at night. Hungry, penniless, and depressed, he fell back on his old hobby of sketching to earn food, exchanging drawings for a crust of bread. He had reached a major turning point in his life.

▲ This French periodical reports a miners' strike during the period when van Gogh was living in the mining community of the Borinage. Van Gogh supported the miners' cause and helped them with gifts of food and clothing.

Learning to Be an Artist

In March of 1880, van Gogh made an important journey. He walked 43 miles (70 km) to visit a leading artist, Jules Breton (1827-1906), to show him his drawings. When he got there he was too shy to knock on the artist's door. However, in a letter to Theo, van Gogh says that on the long walk back home, even without seeing Breton, he decided to become a painter: "I will go on with my drawing. From that moment everything has seemed transformed for me."

◀ *Larener Woman With a Goat*, c.1885, Anton Mauve. Anton Mauve specialized in painting rural scenes. Mauve, like most artists of the time produced paintings that copied elements of the styles of great painters of the past.

A FORMAL EDUCATION

During the nineteenth century, people thought that learning to be an artist required a very formal education. Would-be artists either studied in the studio of an established artist or at an art school for a number of years. If a student chose to study with one particular artist he or she usually learned the artist's style and agreed with their ideas about art. The most famous art school in Europe at the time was the Ecole des Beaux-Arts (School of Fine Arts) in Paris. Students here drew from models three times a week, as well as from plaster casts of the human body. They also visited the Louvre Museum and copied the work of the Old Masters. Most artists were trained to copy the famous artists of the past, and they were graded on their ability to do so – not for creating original work. Even the Impressionists (see page 14), who broke new ground in art, went through this very traditional training.

TIMELINE ▶

1880	1881	1882	1883	1884-85	March 26, 1885
Van Gogh decides to become an artist. Enrolls at Brussels Art Academy and studies under Anton van Rappard.	Van Gogh moves to The Hague, where he studies under Anton Mauve.	Van Gogh lives with Sien Hoornik in The Hague.	Van Gogh paints in Drenthe, then returns to his parents' home in Nuenen.	Van Gogh paints in Nuenen.	Van Gogh's father dies of a stroke.

VAN GOGH STUDIES

In October of 1880 van Gogh enrolled at the Brussels Art Academy, where a wealthy painter named Anton van Rappard (1858-92) helped him. Van Gogh studied anatomy and developed his drawing by copying famous paintings. He also learned the rules of perspective, which artists use to help them draw three-dimensional scenes on flat paper or canvas. In 1881 van Gogh moved back to The Hague to study under Anton Mauve (1838-88), another successful artist. Van Gogh concentrated on drawing and watercolors.

▲ A photograph of one of the many canals of The Hague in the 1880s.

"I shall be poor; I shall be a painter; I want to remain human."

Vincent van Gogh

In 1882 van Gogh began painting in oils on canvas – which quickly became his favorite way of working. Theo sent van Gogh money which he used to pay for models and artists' materials. He lived on a diet of bread and coffee, and was often ill.

While in The Hague, van Gogh moved in with Sien Hoornik, a poor woman who acted as his model, but his parents disapproved of this relationship. Van Gogh eventually gave in and left Sien, Mauve, and The Hague. He rejected what he had learned during his short period of formal training as an artist. He spent a few months painting in the north of the Netherlands, at Drenthe, then went to live with his parents in Nuenen. Van Gogh was still there when his father died of a stroke in March of 1885.

▲ *In the Orchard,* 1883. In Drenthe and Nuenen, van Gogh mainly painted scenes of poor people at work and at home. His ambition now was to make many paintings on this theme – to become a "peasant painter."

The First Major Work

In 1885, while still at Nuenen, van Gogh planned his first major work, *The Potato Eaters* (opposite). He wanted to show a poor farming family at home, sharing a supper of cooked potatoes. The artist, now 32, made many pencil sketches and oil studies of his subject before he began the actual work.

▲ The wash house (laundry) of van Gogh's parents' vicarage at Nuenen. Van Gogh used this building as his studio in the winter of 1883-84.

PAINTING REALITY

Van Gogh was determined not to romanticize the lives of poor farmers, who toiled in the fields from dawn to dusk to grow enough food to survive. Unlike some artists, who painted pretty versions of rural subjects, van Gogh wanted to show the harsh reality of peasant life. He wrote to Theo, "I have tried to emphasize that these people, eating their potatoes in the lamplight, have dug the earth with those very hands they put in the dish … how they have honestly earned their food." Despite all his efforts, however, most people did not like the painting. Discouraged, van Gogh moved to the Belgian city of Antwerp.

▲ *The Frugal Meal*, 1876, Joszef Israels.

PAINTERS OF RURAL LIFE

Many European artists had painted country life and working people before van Gogh. They included the 16th-century Dutch artist Pieter Breugel the Elder (1525-69) and French painter Jean-François Millet (1814-75) whom van Gogh greatly admired. Dutch artists such as Rembrandt and Vermeer (see page 7) were famous for their pictures of interiors. Another artist whom van Gogh looked up to was Joszef Israels (1824-1911). While working at Goupil & Co., van Gogh had seen a print of one of Israels' paintings called *The Frugal Meal* (left). This picture shows peasants eating a simple meal and it inspired *The Potato Eaters*.

TIMELINE ▶

March 1885	November 1885	January 1886
Van Gogh produces his first major works, including *The Potato Eaters*.	Van Gogh moves to Antwerp and tries to meet other artists and sell his work. Buys Japanese prints at the docks which he hangs in his room.	Van Gogh enrolls briefly at Antwerp Art Academy but disagrees with the old-fashioned teaching methods and leaves after a few months.

The Potato Eaters, 1885

oil on canvas, 32 x 45 in (81.5 x 114.5 cm), Rijksmuseum Vincent van Gogh, Vincent van Gogh Foundation, Amsterdam, The Netherlands

Van Gogh painted this farming family in dark, earthy colors, mostly greys, browns and blacks, reflecting their daily work in the fields. He used warmer orange tones to show the soft lamplight which bathes the table where the family sit at their simple meal.

"If a peasant picture smells of bacon, smoke, potato steam – all right, that's not unhealthy."

Vincent van Gogh

The Impressionists

In February of 1886, van Gogh left Antwerp and moved to Paris, where his brother Theo was now a successful art-dealer. The French capital was the center of the art world and home to a new inspiring art movement called Impressionism.

MEETING OTHER ARTISTS

Through Theo, van Gogh met the leading Impressionist artists, including Claude Monet (1840-1926), Camille Pissarro (1830-1903), Pierre-Auguste Renoir (1841-1919), Paul Signac (1863-1935), Emile Bernard (1868-1941), Paul Gauguin (1848-1903), and Henri de Toulouse-Lautrec (1864-1901). Van Gogh and Theo lived in the Montmartre district of Paris, which had become popular with artists because of its cheap housing. Van Gogh was amazed by the bright colors and

▲ *The Bathers, Asnieres*, **1883-84, Georges Seurat.** *The Bathers is made up of thousands of dots of unmixed color.*

freshness of Impressionist paintings. Under their influence, his art underwent a dramatic change. Van Gogh abandoned both his dark colors and his chosen subject of poor working people. Instead he began to paint bright, colorful urban landscapes which included cafés and still-life paintings, just as the Impressionists did.

▲ *Impression, Sunrise*, **1872, Claude Monet.**

IMPRESSIONISM AND POINTILLISM

The Impressionist movement began around 1870, fifteen years before van Gogh arrived in Paris. The movement got its name from a painting by the artist Claude Monet, called *Impression, Sunrise* (left). Impressionist artists often painted in the open air, and worked quickly to try to capture the mood and quality of light at a particular time of day. By 1885, the young artists Georges Seurat (1859-91) and Paul Signac had already moved beyond Impressionism to invent a new technique called Pointillism. They built up their paintings by daubing thousands of flecks of pure color onto the canvas. Van Gogh learned lessons from this method, too.

Moulin de Blute-fin, Montmartre, 1886

oil on canvas, 18 ¹/₃ x 15 in (46.5 x 38 cm), Bridgestone Museum of Art, Tokyo, Japan

In van Gogh's day, the hilltop district of Montmartre in Paris was not built up as it is today, but still looked quite rural. Van Gogh painted several pictures of Montmartre's windmills and the small plots of land where people grew vegetables. This painting reflects the light, airy freshness of Impressionist art.

Japanese Art

▲ *Ukiyo Nijushiko*, Keisai Eisen.

In Paris, van Gogh made friends with a paint merchant named Père Tanguy, whom he painted several times against a background of Japanese prints (see left). These prints were very popular with artists in Europe, including the Impressionists. Van Gogh himself had become enthusiastic about Japanese art while living in Antwerp in 1885. These cheap prints were used as packing material to wrap porcelain and other fragile cargo from Asia, which arrived at ports such as Antwerp. It was from here that van Gogh obtained several prints. He admired their simple colors and bold drawing style.

AN EXHIBITION

In 1887, another of van Gogh's friends, the café-owner Agostina Segatori, allowed him to put on an exhibition of Japanese prints in her café. Later van Gogh showed some of his own work there, along with paintings by other young artists, but none of his pictures sold.

COLOR AND LINE

The work of Japanese printmakers such as Katsushika Hokusai (1760-1849), Keisai Eisen (1790-1848), and Ando Hiroshige (1797-1858) were popular with many artists of van Gogh's day, including Claude Monet. European painters admired the unusual compositions of Japanese prints and their simple blocks of pure color. Van Gogh made several copies of Japanese prints as well as putting them in the background of his portrait of Pere Tanguy. Inspired by Japanese art, he began to draw pictures from unusual viewpoints, and to include areas of flat, plain color, outlined with dark lines.

▲ A café in Paris, 1880s, around the time van Gogh was in the city. Cafés were popular meeting places for artists and writers who wished to discuss their work.

TIMELINE ▶

January-March 1887	Spring 1887	November 1887
Van Gogh puts on an exhibition of Japanese prints at Café du Tambourin, and later shows his own work along with paintings by other young artists, but fails to sell any pictures.	Van Gogh buys some more Japanese prints at a gallery in Paris.	Van Gogh meets Georges Seurat, the founder of the Pointillist school.

Père Tanguy, 1887-88

oil on canvas, 25 $\frac{1}{2}$ x 20 in (65 x 51 cm), Collection Stavros S. Niarchos

Père Tanguy was one of van Gogh's art suppliers in Paris. He sometimes helped young artists by exchanging paint and canvases for finished paintings, and he did this for van Gogh. Van Gogh's portrait of Père Tanguy reflects the old man's generosity and good humor.

South to the Land of Light

▲ *Montagne Sainte-Victoire, 1886-87,* **Paul Cézanne.** Cézanne painted this mountain many times.

INSPIRATIONAL LIGHT

Van Gogh thought the clean air and gusty winds of southern France cleared his head and made his senses more acute. Many other artists agreed, finding inspiration in the clear light and beautiful landscape of the south.

Paul Cézanne (1839-1906), spent most of his life painting in the south of France. Cézanne began his artistic career as an Impressionist, but later developed his own style. He is often called "the father of modern art." Fellow-Impressionist Pierre-Auguste Renoir was based in the south, and a little later, the Mediterranean coast inspired a group called the Fauves (see page 41).

By autumn 1887, van Gogh was becoming tired of the hectic pace of life in Paris – he had painted over 200 pictures in two years. Too many late nights and too much coffee and alcohol were making him ill and irritable. Even Theo found his brother difficult to live with. Fellow artist Toulouse-Lautrec recommended the area of Provence in southern France as a good place to rest and paint. Van Gogh became convinced that the move would restore his health and peace of mind.

MOVING SOUTH

In February of 1888, van Gogh moved to Arles, an ancient town just 16 miles (25 km) from the Mediterranean coast. He arrived to find a snow-covered landscape that reminded him of Japanese prints of winter. As spring came, the almond, cherry, and peach trees burst into blossom, another favorite theme of Japanese painters. "I feel I am in Japan," he wrote.

▲ **A modern replica of the bridge that van Gogh painted at Langlois, near Arles.**

DAZZLING COLOR

As spring turned to summer, van Gogh explored the countryside looking for good locations in which to paint. He was inspired by the dazzling colors of the landscape and completed many canvases in quick succession. He began to develop his own unmistakable style, using bright colors and outlining forms clearly, often with lines of dark color. Van Gogh's energetic brushstrokes complemented his astonishing colors and created a feeling of movement in his paintings.

TIMELINE ▶

February 1888	February 1888	March 1888
Van Gogh and Theo visit Seurat at his studio. Van Gogh leaves Paris for Arles and rents a room near the station.	Van Gogh paints lots of pictures of flowers and trees bursting into life – they remind him of pictures of Japanese landscapes.	Van Gogh's work is shown at the Salon des Indépendants in Paris but doesn't sell.

Langlois Bridge at Arles With Road Alongside the Canal, 1888

oil on canvas, 23 ^{2}/$_5$ x 29 ^{1}/$_8$ in (59.5 x 74 cm), Rijksmuseum Vincent van Gogh, Vincent van Gogh Foundation, Amsterdam, The Netherlands

This little bridge over a canal near Arles became a favorite spot for van Gogh, and he made several paintings of it. Bridges were also a popular theme in Japanese art. Van Gogh had started to sign his paintings "Vincent"– a habit he continued all his life.

"The air here certainly does me good."

Vincent van Gogh

An Artist's Studio

During his first months in Arles, van Gogh lived in a hotel near the railroad station. In May of 1888, he rented rooms in a nearby building, called the Yellow House because of its bright-yellow walls. The apartment had no furniture, so at first van Gogh used it as a studio. He dreamed of making the Yellow House the center of an artists' colony. With this in mind, he invited the painter Paul Gauguin, whom he had met in Paris, to come and stay in Arles.

SYMBOL OF THE SOUTH

In August of 1888, van Gogh began a series of sunflower paintings to decorate the Yellow House for Gauguin's arrival. To van Gogh, these bright yellow flowers were a symbol of the south. "Yellow is the embodiment … of love," he wrote to Theo.

The same color shone out in the cornfields and haystacks, in the fertile soil and in the fiery southern sun. All summer, van Gogh worked at a feverish pace to attain a "high yellow note." Over the next 15 months, he completed 200 paintings, many of them his greatest works.

▲ *Vincent van Gogh Painting Sunflowers*, 1888, **Paul Gauguin.** Gauguin painted this picture while staying with van Gogh (see page 22).

PAINTING IN OILS

Van Gogh had now mastered the use of oil paint, the most popular paint of his day. These paints are made by mixing brightly colored pigments, made from crushed minerals or plants, with linseed oil. Many artists make oil paints thinner by adding turpentine but van Gogh liked to use his oils thick, straight from the tube. Theo sent van Gogh's materials to him all the way from Paris. The artist's letters to Theo are full of requests for more paint.

▲ *Vincent's House in Arles*, **1888.** Van Gogh rented four rooms in the Yellow House for 15 francs a month. He wrote to Theo about the house, "it's terrific, these houses yellow in the sun, and the incomparable freshness of the blue. And all the ground is yellow too."

TIMELINE ▶

May 1888	June 1888	August 1888
Van Gogh rents one half of the Yellow House in Arles, but only uses it as a studio. He lives at the station café run by the Ginoux family.	Van Gogh visits Les Saintes-Maries-de-la-Mer, by the Mediterranean Sea. He makes studies of the boats on the beach. Gauguin agrees to come and see van Gogh in Arles.	Van Gogh meets Joseph Roulin, a postman. They become friends. Van Gogh sends 36 paintings to Theo in Paris. Paints the *Sunflowers* series in preparation for Gauguin's arrival.

Vase With Fourteen Sunflowers, 1888

oil on canvas, 36 $^{3}/_{5}$ x 28 $^{3}/_{4}$ in (93 x 73 cm), National Gallery London, England

Today van Gogh's *Sunflowers* series are among the most famous paintings in the world. In 1987, *Vase With Fourteen Sunflowers* (above) sold for $39.5 million at auction – the highest price that had ever been paid for a painting at that time.

"I am thinking of decorating my studio with half a dozen paintings of sunflowers."

Vincent van Gogh

A Visit From Gauguin

▲ A photograph of Paul Gauguin, paintbrush in hand, c.1890.

PAUL GAUGUIN

Gauguin had been working with other artists in northern France before he went to stay in Arles. He had been introduced to van Gogh by Theo, who was his art dealer in Paris. Theo sent Gauguin a sum of money every month in exchange for pictures, just as he did with van Gogh.

After Gauguin left Arles, he visited Tahiti, an island in the Pacific Ocean, and later went to live there permanently. Gauguin usually painted from memory, and used color to express emotion in his paintings.

In September of 1888, van Gogh bought furniture for the Yellow House using money sent by Theo. He moved in and did several paintings of his bedroom (below), which he loved for its bright colors and peaceful atmosphere. Gauguin arrived in October. Van Gogh was delighted to have a companion to paint with and to discuss ideas about art. His dream of a "studio in the south" was at last coming true.

▲ *Vincent's Bedroom in Arles*, 1880. Van Gogh's picture shows his bedroom to be a neat and cheerful place uncluttered by possessions, with some of his favorite paintings on the wall.

The two artists went out together to paint local scenes. They visited a museum in Montpellier, a nearby town, to study the art collection there. At first, van Gogh and Gauguin got along well, but after a few weeks differences in their characters and their approaches to painting began to cause arguments and the atmosphere became tense.

TIMELINE ▶

September 1888	October 23, 1888	December 1888
Van Gogh moves into his half of the Yellow House. He has four rooms to himself and dreams of setting up an artists' colony.	Gauguin comes to stay with van Gogh. In the weeks that follow Gauguin and van Gogh work together and talk about art.	Van Gogh and Gauguin visit the museum in the nearby town of Montpellier. They see, and are inspired by, works by Eugène Delacroix (1798-1863) and Gustave Courbet (1819-77).

Paul Gauguin's Armchair, 1888

oil on canvas, 35 5/8 x 28 1/2 in (90.5 x 72.5 cm), Rijksmuseum Vincent van Gogh, Vincent van Gogh Foundation, Amsterdam, The Netherlands

During Gauguin's stay, van Gogh painted pictures of two chairs, his own and the one Gauguin used. Van Gogh meant the two paintings to express the differences in their characters. Van Gogh's chair was a simple seat – the chair of a "peasant painter." Gauguin's chair, with its curving arms and firmly planted legs, seems to reflect Gauguin's greater confidence.

"Gauguin is very powerful, strongly creative ..."

Vincent van Gogh

Breakdown

Van Gogh and Gauguin had different ideas about art and used different methods for painting. Gauguin often painted from memory, whereas van Gogh liked to paint from real life. Gauguin was more self-confident and was convinced his way was better. He mocked van Gogh for working too realistically. The two painters began to argue.

▲ A photograph of Theo van Gogh, taken in 1889. Theo believed in his brother's talent as an artist and was deeply affected by the breakdown in van Gogh's health. In turn, van Gogh was upset that Theo had to be called away from Paris to help him in Arles.

OVERWORKING

All summer, van Gogh had been working hard, but neglected to look after himself properly. He had been eating too little and drinking too much. He often painted all night because he could not sleep, and for months he drove himself to complete a huge number of paintings. "One must strike while the iron is hot," he wrote to Theo. "To attain the high yellow note I achieved last summer, I had to be pretty well keyed up." Van Gogh's physical and mental health both began to suffer. He developed stomach pains and fainting fits which gradually became more frequent.

"If he had found someone to whom he could have opened his heart, perhaps it would never have gone this far."

Theo van Gogh

GROWING PROBLEMS

Meanwhile, the arguments between van Gogh and Gauguin became worse. "Our arguments are terribly electric, we come out of them sometimes with our heads as exhausted as an electric battery after it has run down," van Gogh wrote to Theo. He added, "I must beware of my nerves." Gauguin found van Gogh chaotic and over-emotional, and he began to fear van Gogh's fiery temper. In turn, van Gogh found Gauguin bossy and critical.

TIMELINE ▶

December 1888	December 24	January 7, 1889
Theo becomes engaged to Johanna (Jo) Bonger. December 23 van Gogh has a mental crisis and threatens Gauguin. Depressed, he later cuts off part of his ear.	Unconscious, van Gogh is taken to Arles hospital. Theo arrives from Paris the following day.	After two weeks van Gogh is released from the hospital. He writes to his family that he is better and that they are not to worry about him.

In December of 1888, Theo wrote to van Gogh with important news. Theo was engaged to be married to a young Dutch woman, Johanna Bonger (1862-1925). Van Gogh may have felt that Theo's marriage would make his own relationship with his brother more distant or he may even have felt betrayed. On top of his difficult relationship with Gauguin the strain proved too much.

A MENTAL CRISIS

On the evening of December 23, just before Christmas, van Gogh and Gauguin had a violent quarrel. Van Gogh threatened Gauguin and Gauguin fled, spending the night in a boarding house. Alone at the Yellow House, van Gogh became more and more upset. In desperation, he cut off part of his ear, wandered outside and gave it to a local woman he knew. The horrified woman told the police.

▲ At Arles hospital, van Gogh was put under the care of a local doctor, Félix Rey (1867-1932). Van Gogh painted this portrait of Rey in appreciation for the care he took of him during his mental illness.

▼ The hospital in Arles where van Gogh was taken after his mental breakdown in December of 1888. Van Gogh later painted and drew this courtyard several times.

In the morning, the police found van Gogh exhausted and unconscious in his bed. They took him to the local hospital, where he remained unconscious for another three days. Gauguin telephoned Theo to tell him of van Gogh's condition. Theo rushed to van Gogh's bedside. Within just a few days, van Gogh seemed to recover. "I hope I just had simply an artist's fit," he wrote to Theo later.

On January 7, 1889, van Gogh was allowed to go home. Theo returned to Paris, and Gauguin left Arles. Gauguin explained to Theo: "Vincent and I cannot live together without trouble; our characters are incompatible."

A Troubled Mind

▲ *The Absinthe Drinkers*, 1876, Edgar Degas. Absinthe was a popular drink in France in the nineteenth century.

THE MADNESS OF VAN GOGH

Over the years, doctors have tried to discover more about van Gogh's mental illness. Some medical experts think his condition may have been hereditary since there was a history of mental illness in the family (one of van Gogh's sisters spent most of her life in a mental hospital).

Other doctors think van Gogh's health was affected by drinking absinthe, a cheap, strong spirit which was later banned in France because it caused brain damage.

Van Gogh himself believed his illness was due to his poor physical condition. "I am beginning to consider madness a disease like any other," he wrote.

Van Gogh was back in the Yellow House but now it seemed empty. Friends called in from time to time, but he was mostly alone. Van Gogh wrote to Theo that "whole days pass without my speaking to anyone." Forced to be independent, van Gogh began painting again. Among the first paintings completed after his mental crisis were several self-portraits.

LOOKING IN THE MIRROR

Over the years, van Gogh had often painted himself, partly because he had no other model. Painting by looking at his own face in the mirror may have helped him feel calmer. In some of his self-portraits, such as the picture below, van Gogh looks sad or troubled. In others he looks fairly cheerful. The picture opposite was made soon after his release from the hospital. He has included his easel and a Japanese print in the background to highlight two of the things that make him happy.

◀ *Self-Portrait Dedicated to Paul Gauguin*, 1888. In this painting van Gogh looks sad and haunted. There is no escape from his troubled eyes, made more intense by his close-shaved head and bony skull.
No objects are painted in the background of the picture so the viewer is forced to focus on van Gogh.

TIMELINE ▶

January 1889	January 1889	January 1889
After his release from hospital van Gogh spends time alone at the Yellow House. He begins painting again, including self-portraits.	Van Gogh paints *Self-Portrait with Bandaged Ear* and *Portrait of Dr. Félix Rey* (see page 25).	Van Gogh writes to Theo asking him to send Gauguin his best wishes.

Self-Portrait With Bandaged Ear, 1889

oil on canvas, 23 ³/5 x 19 ¹/4 in (60 x 49 cm), Courtauld Institute
Galleries, London, England

Van Gogh painted this self-portrait in January of 1889, not long after his
release from hospital. In all, he painted around 40 self-portraits between
1885 and 1889. His left ear was the damaged one, but because he
painted this picture by looking in a mirror, the image was reversed so it
appears to be his right ear that is hurt.

*"Working on my
pictures is almost a
necessity for my
recovery."*

Vincent van Gogh

A Good Friend

PORTRAIT PAINTER

During his time in Arles, van Gogh painted dozens of portraits. Many were of friends such as Augustine Roulin. In about 1888, under Gauguin's influence, van Gogh began to use color to express emotion in his pictures. He told Theo, "I want to paint men and women with something of the eternal, which I am trying to convey through the radiance … of my coloring." Around this time, he felt he was learning "a great lesson taught by the old Dutch masters … to consider drawing and color as one."

▲ A photograph of Arles around the time that van Gogh lived there. Arles has always been a popular vacation destination thanks to the town's ancient Roman remains, and its quaint streets, cafés, and shops.

During this troubled time, van Gogh was visited regularly by a good friend, Joseph Roulin. He was a large man that worked for the post office unloading mail at the railroad station. He also lived near the Yellow House. Van Gogh painted several portraits of Roulin, and also of his wife Augustine, their teenage son Armand, and even their baby, Marcelle. Roulin and his wife supported the artist during the dark days of January 1889, but then the postman was transferred to the city of Marseille. After they had left, van Gogh painted more copies of their portraits.

▲ *Mother Roulin With Her Baby*, 1888. Joseph Roulin's wife, Augustine, was one of van Gogh's favorite subjects.

ILL AGAIN

Early in February, van Gogh had another mental crisis and began to hallucinate, or see things that were not there. The people of Arles were alarmed by van Gogh's behavior and signed a petition to have him locked away. When another attack came in late February, van Gogh was hospitalized. The "artist's fit," began to return regularly.

TIMELINE ▶

February 4, 1889	February 27, 1889	March 1889
Van Gogh suffers another breakdown – he is convinced that someone is trying to poison him. This lasts for two weeks.	Van Gogh has another attack, is taken back to hospital. In between attacks he works at the Yellow House.	Van Gogh suffers his fourth attack. Thirty of his neighbors sign a petition asking to have him committed to hospital permanently. The townspeople give him a nickname: the redheaded madman. The police close up the Yellow House with all of van Gogh's work inside.

The Postman Roulin, 1889

oil on canvas, 25 3/5 x 21 1/4 in (65 x 54 cm), Rijksmuseum Kroller-Muller Otterlo, The Netherlands

Van Gogh wrote to Theo, "Roulin ... is not old enough to be like a father to me, nevertheless he has a tenderness, such as an old soldier might have for a young one." Van Gogh's portrait captures the postman's kindly nature.

"What appeals to me most is the portrait, the modern portrait."

Vincent van Gogh

Painting Through the Night

▲ The asylum at Saint-Rémy is still a mental hospital.

ASYLUMS

In asylums such as Saint-Rémy, patients such as van Gogh enjoyed more privacy than they would have on a ward in a public hospital. Van Gogh had his own room, plus another room to paint in.

During his attacks of depression – which sometimes lasted for days – he was locked up, but at other times he was allowed to wander the asylum grounds and the surrounding countryside. Ideas about mental illness were very primitive in the nineteenth century, as were most treatments. Patients like van Gogh, who were diagnosed as having epilepsy, were treated with cold baths. Van Gogh wrote: "You continually hear terrible cries and howls like beasts in a zoo."

Theo and Jo were married in April of 1889. Soon after, van Gogh suffered another attack and had to return to the hospital. However, there was no privacy on the public ward at Arles and a local priest suggested he should transfer to the asylum, or mental hospital, at the nearby town of Saint-Rémy, where conditions would be better. In May of 1889, van Gogh went to Saint-Rémy voluntarily. He stayed there for a year.

MADNESS AND MASTERPIECES

Van Gogh's attacks continued, but in between, he copied his favorite prints and paintings and made still-life studies. He also painted the view from his room, even at night (see opposite). Van Gogh created many masterpieces during his time at Saint-Rémy. He felt that painting helped soothe and heal his spirit, but he continued to drive himself too hard. The emotional strain of completing a series of great paintings quickly may have helped trigger his attacks of illness and depression.

◄ *The Café Terrace on the Place du Forum, Arles, at Night*, 1888. "The problem of painting at night interests me tremendously," wrote van Gogh. When working outdoors in dim light van Gogh stuck candles on the brim of his hat and on his easel to help him see. Van Gogh's night pictures are always full of color and light, and are never gloomy.

TIMELINE ▶

April 1889	May 1889	1889
On April 17 Theo and Johanna Bonger marry in Amsterdam. Soon after, van Gogh has another attack.	Van Gogh enters the asylum of Saint Paul at Saint-Rémy as a voluntary patient and stays there for a year. He begins to feel calmer and is allowed to paint and draw.	In July, van Gogh has another attack and tries to swallow his paints which are poisonous. He has another attack in December and tries to do the same thing again.

Starry Night, 1889
oil on canvas, 29 x 36 $^1/_4$ in (73.7 x 92.1 cm), Museum of Modern Art, New York, New York

Van Gogh painted *Starry Night* from behind the bars of the window in his room in the asylum at Saint-Rémy. In the vast starlit sky, van Gogh told Theo he glimpsed "something one can only call God ... eternity in its place above this world." The stars in this painting glow with brilliant swirls of color. Yet the painting also accurately shows the constellations and planets that shone in the night sky in June of 1889, the month van Gogh painted the picture.

"In the blue depths the stars were sparkling, greenish, yellow, white, pink, more brilliant ... than at home, even in Paris."

Vincent van Gogh

Return to the North

▲ Claude Monet was one of the leading Impressionist artists – to be complimented by him was an honor.

PRAISE AT LAST

In 1888, 1889, and 1890, van Gogh's paintings appeared at the Salon des Indépendants, an annual exhibition of modern artists in Paris. In 1890, his work earned high praise. Paul Gauguin reported to van Gogh, "Monet said your paintings were best of all... Many artists felt you were the most remarkable one in the exhibition." In January of 1890, a poet called Albert Aurier (1865-92) published an article which also praised van Gogh's work. In March of 1890, one of van Gogh's paintings, *The Red Vineyard*, was sold. At last van Gogh's work was becoming known.

▲ *The Red Vineyard*, 1888, was the only painting van Gogh sold during his lifetime. It was bought for 400 francs – at the time a very good price.

Van Gogh wrote to Theo from Saint-Rémy, telling him, "During my illness, I saw again every room in the house at Zundert, every path, every plant in the garden." As time passed, he missed northern Europe more and more. In 1890 he decided to travel back to the north of France.

In January, Theo's wife Jo had given birth to a baby son, who had been named Vincent. In May, van Gogh left the south and traveled to Paris to visit Theo. For the first time he was able to meet Jo and the baby. After a few days in Paris, van Gogh traveled on to the village of Auvers-sur-Oise, north of Paris, where Theo knew of a psychiatrist, Paul Gachet (1828-1909), who could look after his brother. Van Gogh rented a room above a local café and saw Dr. Gachet and his family regularly. The countryside around Auvers was inspiring, and he began another period of intense activity, painting a picture every day for 70 days.

TIMELINE ▶

January 1890	February 22, 1890	March 1890	May 1890
January 31 Johanna van Gogh gives birth to a baby son, who is named Vincent. An article by Albert Aurier praising van Gogh's work appears in *Mercure de France*, a French journal.	Van Gogh falls mentally ill again. This lasts for two months.	Van Gogh's painting *The Red Vinyard* sells for 400 francs.	May 17 van Gogh goes to Paris for a three-day visit to see Theo and his family. May 20 goes to live in Auvers-sur-Oise, 19 miles (30 km) north of Paris.

The Church at Auvers, 1890
oil on canvas, 37 x 29 1/8 in (94 x 74 cm), Musée d'Orsay, Paris, France

Van Gogh painted *The Church at Auvers*, deliberately distorting the perspective of the picture. The painting is unified by strong, flowing lines and rhythmic swirls of paint that make the big, solid stone church dance with movement.

"I am in a continual fever of work."

Vincent van Gogh

In the Care of Dr. Gachet

As well as being a doctor, Paul Gachet was also an amateur artist and an art-lover. Paintings by Claude Monet and Paul Cézanne decorated his home, and he knew many of the Impressionist artists (see page 14) from his days as a medical student in Paris. The artists Camille Pissarro and Pierre-Auguste Renoir were in his care, as well as van Gogh. Gachet's love of art and his unconventional ideas meant that he had many things in common with van Gogh. The two men became friends.

A GOOD DOCTOR

Van Gogh ate most of his meals at the café where he was lodging, but he also regularly dined at the Gachets'. He made several portraits of the doctor and his daughter. Even van Gogh found Gachet eccentric: "He is as disorganized about his work as a doctor as I am about my painting," he told Theo. Yet with the psychiatrist's help, van Gogh was able to relax and work steadily.

▲ A foxglove appears in Dr. Gachet's portrait to symbolize his homeopathic skills.

HOMEOPATHIC MEDICINE

Paul Gachet was unusual for his time because he was a doctor who practiced homeopathy. This branch of medicine requires expert knowledge of the healing properties of hundreds of different minerals and plants. Homeopathic doctors give their patients tiny quantities of plant or mineral remedies, which stimulate the body's own defences against illness. The soft, wrinkled leaves of the foxglove contain digitalis which can be used as a heart tonic.

◀ This photograph of Dr. Gachet's house was taken during the 1980s. Van Gogh went there frequently to paint and have dinner with the family as well as to receive treatment. "I feel I cannot do a bad painting every time I go to his house," he wrote.

TIMELINE ▶

May 1890	May 1890
Van Gogh makes friends with Dr. Paul Gachet and his two children, Marguerite (age 20) and Paul (age 16).	Van Gogh paints pictures of the village and the surrounding countryside.

Portrait of Dr. Gachet, 1890
oil on canvas, 26 2/5 x 22 in (67 x 56 cm), Private Collection

Van Gogh painted Paul Gachet's portrait in June 1890. The psychiatrist was so enthusiastic about the result that he asked the artist to paint a copy for him, too.

"I am working with calm and steady enthusiasm."

Vincent van Gogh

Under Threatening Skies

From Auvers van Gogh wrote to Theo saying that he was "... working much and fast, in that way I try to express the desperately rapid passing of things in modern life." The artist's routine was demanding: he was usually up by 5 A.M. to go out on a painting expedition. He worked outside in sunshine, wind, and rain.

BRILLIANT INSANITY

In letters to Theo, van Gogh compared his present work with paintings he had done previously. "I feel much surer of my brushstrokes than before going to Arles," he wrote. In the space of just ten years, van Gogh's skills had advanced greatly, and he now had the sure touch of a master.

▲ This detail of the crows in *Landscape at Auvers in the Rain* (opposite) shows van Gogh's forceful brushmarks.

The landscapes he painted at Auvers are beautiful, but their dark colors and violent brushstrokes suggest that he was gripped by a great inner struggle. The drive to work at such great speed was now threatening his sanity.

▲ A field of sunflowers in Provence.

SYMBOLS IN VAN GOGH'S WORK

Van Gogh's work features images which some people think are symbols. Sunflowers seem to symbolize the hot south of France, happiness, love, and van Gogh's time of hope in the Yellow House at Arles. In the summer of 1890, van Gogh painted a series of landscapes featuring cloudy or rainy skies and flying crows. Many people see these images as symbols of the artist's distressed mental state. The dark, twisting poplar trees that appear in some of van Gogh's later paintings are also menacing shapes that could symbolize his desperate struggle against mental illness.

TIMELINE ▶

June 1890	June 1890
Dr. Gachet visits Theo in Paris and tells him that he thinks his brother has made a full recovery.	Van Gogh paints constantly. With the encouragement of Dr. Gachet he tries etching for the first time.

Landscape at Auvers in the Rain, 1890

oil on canvas, 19 2/3 x 39 3/8 in (50 x 100 cm), National Museum of Wales, Cardiff, Wales

Van Gogh painted *Landscape at Auvers in the Rain* in July 1890. He wrote: "These are vast stretches of corn under threatening skies, and I need not go out of my way to express sadness and extreme loneliness." In the paintings he made in the summer of 1890, van Gogh's brushmarks became even stronger. The diagonal lines that streak over *Landscape at Auvers in the Rain* look like black scars on the canvas.

"... perhaps there is a purpose in pain, which, when viewed from here, sometimes dominates the horizon so completely that it looks like a hopeless flood to us. We know very little about how these things are related, and we do better to look at a cornfield, even if it is only painted."

Vincent van Gogh

Final Days

▲ The café Ravoux, where Vincent spent the last months of his life. His attic room overlooked the town hall in Auvers.

By July of 1890, van Gogh felt overwhelmed by troubles. In June, Theo, Jo, and the baby visited Auvers, and the four went on a picnic. During the visit, Theo told his brother of his own problems at work and at home, where the baby was often sick. Theo seemed weighed down by responsibility. Van Gogh wrote to him, "I … feel the storm which threatens you weighing on me also. I generally try to be cheerful, but my life too is threatened at the very root, and my steps are wavering."

Van Gogh's friendship with Dr. Gachet had also cooled. On a visit to Gachet's house, the artist became angry because the doctor had not framed some of the paintings he owned, which lay stacked against the walls. Van Gogh flew into a rage, threatened Gachet with a pistol, and then ran away, horror-stricken at what he had done.

"There are many things I should like to write you about, but I feel it is useless."

Vincent van Gogh

TIMELINE ▶

June 8, 1890	July 6, 1890	July 27, 1890	July 29, 1890	January 15, 1891
Theo and family visit van Gogh in Auvers.	Van Gogh visits Theo in Paris, learns of his plans to move back to the Netherlands.	Van Gogh shoots himself in the chest in an attempt to commit suicide.	Van Gogh dies of his injuries at the age of 37.	Theo van Gogh dies of bronchitis and other illnesses, at age 34.

AN ATTEMPT AT SUICIDE

On July 6, van Gogh visited Theo in Paris and saw some of his old artist friends. He returned to Auvers in distress. Theo had told him that he and Jo were planning to return to the Netherlands, and van Gogh may have felt abandoned. On July 27, 1890, the misery became unbearable. He went out into the fields with a pistol and shot himself in the chest. Fortunately the bullet only injured him. He struggled back to Auvers and limped up to his room.

A FATAL INJURY

The innkeeper with whom he was staying became suspicious when van Gogh did not come down for supper. He went to van Gogh's room and found the artist bleeding on his bed. A doctor was called, but could not help. The bullet had missed van Gogh's heart but lodged near his spine. Theo was summoned from Paris and arrived early the next morning. The brothers spent many hours alone before van Gogh died in Theo's arms. He was just 37 years old.

▲ Dr. Gachet made this sketch of van Gogh's face soon after he died.

"I wish it were all over now."

Vincent van Gogh's last words

A SMALL FUNERAL

Some of van Gogh's old friends came to the funeral, which took place a few days later. As well as Dr. Gachet and Theo, the artist Emile Bernard was there, and Père Tanguy. "Well, the truth is, we can only make our pictures speak," van Gogh wrote in a final, unsent letter to Theo, found in his pocket. His words were echoed in the speech Dr. Gachet made at his grave: "He was an honest man, and a great artist. He had only two aims, mankind and art. Art he loved above everything, and it will make him live."

▲ Theo van Gogh survived his brother by only a few months. He died in January 1891. At his wife Jo's request, Theo's body was taken to Auvers and buried next to van Gogh. The two brothers were close in death as they had been in life.

Van Gogh's Legacy

In his few short years as an artist van Gogh created over 800 oil paintings and 700 drawings – more than some artists produce in a lifetime of work.

It was only a few years after his death that van Gogh's art began to receive the praise it deserved. In part, this was thanks to Theo's widow, Jo. When Theo died of bronchitis and other illnesses in January of 1891, he had been trying to arrange an exhibition of van Gogh's pictures. Jo carried out the project – and luckily ignored advice to throw the paintings away. Van Gogh's work appeared at the Salon des Indépendants in Paris in March of 1891 and an important art critic, Octave Mirbeau (1848-1917), wrote an enthusiastic review.

PUBLIC RECOGNITION

In May of 1892, less than two years after his death, the first major exhibition of van Gogh's work took place in The Hague. Forty-five paintings were put on show. Again, they attracted praise. As van Gogh's work became better known, an art dealer named Ambroise Vollard (1865-1917) traced friends such as the Roulins and Dr. Rey, and persuaded them to sell the paintings van Gogh had given them. They can now be seen in art galleries around the world. During his lifetime, van Gogh only sold one painting (see page 32). Now his work sells for some of the highest prices ever paid for art.

BOOKS, FILMS, MUSIC

In 1910, an art critic published a study of van Gogh's work – the first of hundreds of books about him. Today, thanks to books, exhibitions, films, operas, poetry, and even pop songs featuring his life and work, van Gogh is one of the world's best-known artists.

◄ *The Scream*, 1893, Edvard Munch. Van Gogh's influence can be seen in Munch's swirling brushstrokes and distorted perspective.

▶ *Fate of the Animals,*
1913, Franz Marc.
Franz Marc (1880-1916)
was part of "Der Blaue
Reiters" (The Blue Riders), a
group of German
Expressionists who were
influenced by van Gogh's
dramatic use of color.

COLOR AND EMOTION

During the 20th century, van Gogh's influence over art and artists reached all across Europe and the U.S. Norwegian artist Edvard Munch (1863-1954), who was part of an art movement called Expressionism, was inspired by van Gogh's skill at conveying emotion. Around 1900, a group of French painters called the "Fauves" (meaning Wild Beasts) were inspired by van Gogh's pictures to use strong colors to express their emotions.

BRUSHWORK AND HONESTY

Simularly, German Expressionists, "Der Blaue Rieters" (The Blue Riders) formed in 1911, were influenced by his bold use of colors. A group of German artists called "Die Brücke" (meaning The Bridge) were influenced by van Gogh's intense colors and use of perspective. Later in the 20th century, van Gogh inspired a huge range of artists worldwide. They imitated his vigorous brushwork, distorted perspective, and vibrant colors. British artist Francis Bacon (1909-92) was influenced by the honesty of van Gogh's self-portraits in his own portraits. Artists such as Renato Guttuso (1911-87) and Jiri Kolar (b.1914) reworked themes by van Gogh to show their appreciation of him.

◀ The Rijksmuseum Vincent van Gogh, in Amsterdam, The Netherlands, was opened in 1973 and is home to a collection of 207 of van Gogh's paintings and nearly 600 of his drawings.

Van Gogh's Letters

Vincent van Gogh lives on not only in his art, but also in his letters. The artist was an excellent letter-writer, who regularly corresponded not only with Theo and other members of his family, such as his mother and sister Willemina, but also with artist friends such as Emile Bernard, Paul Signac, and Paul Gauguin.

WORKS OF ART IN WORDS

Many of van Gogh's letters contain sketches of local scenes or paintings he was working on. As well as writing about his progress and feelings, van Gogh also comments on current events and social issues. A well-read man, he often writes about his favorite authors, who included Shakespeare (1564-1616) and novelists Charles Dickens (1812-70), George Eliot (1819-80), and Emile Zola (1840-1902). In letters to artists such as Gauguin and Emile Bernard, van Gogh shares his ideas about art and discusses the latest developments in painting.

▲ Van Gogh included this sketch of his portrait of Dr. Gachet (see page 35) in a letter to Theo.

"Let's talk about Frans Hals ... Hammer into your head that master Frans Hals, that painter of all kinds of portraits, of a whole, gallant, live immortal republic."

◄ Van Gogh in a letter to Emile Bernard, 1888.

He corresponded regularly with Emile Bernard, whom he met in Paris in 1886. As the older man, van Gogh sometimes offered Bernard advice and recommended the study of masters such as Dutch artist Frans Hals (c.1580-1666).

TIMELINE ▶

1853	1873	1877	1881	1885
March 30, 1853 Vincent van Gogh born in the Netherlands.	**May 1873** Transferred to Goupil's London office.	**May 1877** Studies to read theology at University of Amsterdam but fails the entrance exam.	**1881** Moves to The Hague to study with Anton Mauve.	**November 1885** Moves to Antwerp.
May 1, 1857 Theodorus (Theo) van Gogh born.	**May 1875** Transferred to Goupil's Paris office.	**1878** Studies to enter religious college in Brussels but fails entrance exam.	**1882** Lives with Sien Hoornik.	**January 1886** Briefly attends Antwerp Art Academy.
1861-64 Van Gogh attends the local school.	**January 1876** Dismissed from Goupil & Co.	**December 1878-August 1879** Works as a lay preacher in the Borinage.	**1883** Paints in Drenthe then returns to his parents' home in Nuenen.	**February 1886** Moves to Paris, lives with Theo. Meets the Impressionists.
1864-68 At boarding school.	**April 1876** Works as a teacher in Kent, then in London.	**1880** Decides to become an artist. Attends Brussels Art Academy.	**1884-85** Paints in Nuenen.	**June 1886** Theo and van Gogh move to Montmatre.
July 30, 1869 Starts work at Goupil & Co. in The Hague.	**January-April 1877** Works as a bookshop clerk in Dordecht.		**March 26, 1885** Van Gogh's father dies.	**Winter 1886** Van Gogh meets Paul Gauguin.
			1885 *The Potato Eaters.*	

LETTERS TO THEO

Van Gogh and Theo corresponded throughout their adult lives. Theo carefully kept van Gogh's correspondence. Over 650 letters survive. Van Gogh opened his heart to his brother, pouring out his hopes, fears, and deepest emotions. For example, during his first years as an artist, he spoke of his loneliness:

> *"There may be a great fire in our soul, yet no one ever comes to warm himself at it, and passers-by see only a wisp of smoke."*

As an art dealer living in the French capital, Theo kept van Gogh in touch with developments in the world of art. He sent news of exhibitions and reported all the latest events in Paris. Throughout his adult life, Theo supported van Gogh not only financially, but also emotionally. The artist freely acknowledged his debt to his brother: "If I did not have your friendship, I should be remorselessly driven to suicide, and, cowardly as I am, I should commit it in the end," he wrote in 1889.

LETTERS TO VAN GOGH

Only a few of Theo's letters to van Gogh survive, because the artist did not keep them as carefully. Theo's letters show his affection for his brother. "You have repaid me many times over by your work as well as by your friendship, which is of greater value than all the money I shall ever possess."

Van Gogh's letters are often poetic and even philosophical. They are remarkable writings that reveal his imagination and intelligence. In 1889, van Gogh wrote to Theo:

> *"Looking at the stars always makes me dream ... Why, I ask myself, shouldn't the shining dots of the sky be as accessible as the black dots on the map of France? Just as we take the train to get to Tarascon or Rouen, so we take death to reach a star."*

▲ Van Gogh in a letter to Theo in 1889, around the time he painted *Starry Night* (see page 31).

1887	1888	1888	1889	1890
November 1887 Meets Georges Seurat.	**August 1888** Meets Joseph Roulin. Paints the *Sunflowers* series.	**December 23, 1888** Van Gogh has a mental crisis, cuts off part of his ear.	**March 1889** Fourth attack.	**March 1890** *The Red Vineyard* is sold.
February 1888 Van Gogh leaves Paris for Arles.	**September 1888** Moves into the Yellow House.	**December 24, 1888** Unconscious, van Gogh is taken to Arles hospital. Theo comes from Paris.	**April 17, 1889** Theo marries Johanna (Jo).	**May 20, 1890** Goes to live in Auvers-sur-Oise. Meets Dr. Paul Gachet.
March 1888 Van Gogh's work is shown at the Salon des Indépendants in Paris but doesn't sell.	**October 23, 1888** Gauguin comes to Arles to stay with van Gogh. They live and work together.	**January 7, 1889** Van Gogh is released from hospital and returns to the Yellow House alone.	**May 1889** Van Gogh enters the Saint Paul asylum at Saint-Rémy. Stays for one year.	**July 27, 1890** Van Gogh shoots himself in the chest.
May 1888 Van Gogh rents part of the Yellow House and uses it as a studio.	**December 1888** Theo becomes engaged to Johanna (Jo) Bonger.	**February 1889** Suffers two more attacks.	**July-December 1889** Van Gogh suffers more attacks.	**July 29, 1890** Van Gogh dies of his injuries.
				January 15, 1891 Theo van Gogh dies.

Glossary

anatomy: the study of the human body and how to draw it.

canvas: a woven cloth used as a base for paintings. Materials used include linen, cotton, and hemp, which are treated to stop the paint from sinking too far into the material.

chaotic: making no sense, confused, having no order.

constellations: any of the 88 groups of stars that can be seen from Earth.

Die Brücke: Die Brücke means "The Bridge" in German. Die Brücke was a German Expressionist art movement whose followers tried to reveal the emotional truth of nature rather than just its appearance. Well-known Die Brücke artists include Emil Nolde (1867-1956) and Karl Schmidt-Rottluff (1884-1976).

epilepsy: a medical condition that involves occasional loss of consciousness and/or physical control.

Expressionism: an approach to painting which communicates an emotional state of mind rather than external reality.

Fauves: French for "wild beasts," the name given by a shocked critic in 1905 to a group of painters, including Henri Matisse (1869-1954) and Andre Derain (1880-1954).

flat: in painting, the word flat refers to an area of single, plain color, without varying tones.

hallucination: something which the mind sees or experiences but which does not exist in reality.

homeopathy: a branch of medical treatment which involves giving patients tiny amounts of remedies made from plants or minerals. The remedies stimulate the body's natural defenses against illness.

Impressionism: a group of artists based in Paris during the late 19th century who painted "impressions" of the world with broad brushstrokes of pure color. The group included Pierre-Auguste Renoir (1841-1919), Claude Monet (1840-1926), and Edgar Degas (1834-1917).

incompatible: unable to be put together.

interior: in painting, a picture of an indoor scene. Dutch artists were famous for their interior pictures.

mental illness: an illness of the mind. Mental illness can take many forms and relatively little is known about its treatment and cure.

model: someone who sits still for a period of time so that artists can make a likeness of them.

oil paint: a type of paint made by mixing pigments (made from crushed plants or minerals) with linseed oil. Oil paint can be applied thick, straight from the tube, or it can be diluted, or made thinner.

Old Masters: the greatest European painters during the period 1500-1800, including Leonardo da Vinci (1452-1519), Michelangelo (1475-1564), and Rembrandt (1606-69).

perspective: a set of rules that artists follow to give paintings or drawings done on a flat surface a sense of depth.

Pointillism: an art movement pioneered by French artists Georges Seurat (1859-91) and Paul Signac (1863-1935) during the 1880s. Pointillist paintings are made up of thousands of dots of pure color.

psychiatrist: a doctor who treats mental illness.

still-life: a picture of objects, usually carefully arranged by the artist.

studio: an artist's workshop.

symbols: something, such as an image of an object, that represents something else, such as an idea or an emotion.

Symbolism: an art movement which tried to give ideas, such as love and hate, a visual form in a drawing or on a canvas.

theology: the study of religion.

watercolor: a painting created with colors (called pigments) diluted with water.

Museums and Galleries

Works by van Gogh are exhibited in museums and galleries all around the world. Some of the ones listed here are devoted solely to van Gogh, but most have a wide range of other artists' works on display.

Even if you can't visit any of these galleries yourself, you may be able to visit their web sites. Gallery web sites often show pictures of the artworks they have on display. Some of the web sites even offer virtual tours which allow you to wander around and look at different paintings while sitting comfortably in front of your computer.

Most of the international web sites listed below include an option that allows you to view them in English.

EUROPE

Courtauld Institute of Art
Somerset House
Strand
London WC2R ORN
England UK
www.courtauld.ac.uk

Kröller-Müller Museum
Houtkampweg 6
P.O. Box 1
6730 AA Otterlo
The Netherlands
www.kmm.nl

Louvre Museum
Musée du Louvre
75058 Paris, Cedex 01
France
www.louvre.fr

Musée d'Orsay
Quai Anatole France
Paris 7e
France
www.musee-orsay.fr

Museum of Modern Art
Koingsplein/Place Royale 1-2
1000 Brussels
Belgium
www.fine-arts-museum.be

National Gallery
Trafalgar Square
London WC2N 5DN
England UK
www.nationalgallery.org.uk

Stedelijk Museum
Paulus Potterstraat 13
P.O. Box 75082
1071 AB Amsterdam
The Netherlands
www.stedelijk.nl

Van Gogh Museum
Paulus Potterstraat 7
P.O. Box 75366
1070 AJ Amsterdam
The Netherlands
www.vangoghmuseum.nl

UNITED STATES

Art Institute of Chicago
111 South Michigan Avenue
Chicago, IL 60603
www.artic.edu

Baltimore Museum of Art
10 Art Museum Drive
Baltimore, MD 21218-3898
www.artbma.org

Carnegie Museum of Art
4400 Forbes Avenue
Pittsburgh, PA 15213-4080
www.cmoa.org

Cleveland Museum of Art
11150 East Boulevard
Cleveland, OH 44106-1797
www.clemusart.com

Metropolitan Museum of Art
1000 Fifth Avenue
New York, NY 10028-0198
www.metmuseum.org

Museum of Fine Arts
465 Huntington Avenue
Boston, MA 02115-5523
www.boston.com/mfa/

Index